For my children,
in heaven and on earth,

You inspire me daily and
bring me closer to God. I
love you with my whole heart.

Dear gentle woman,

For you are gentle, though you may not feel it. Even if you feel hardened and numb from your trials and daily tasks, you are gentle. I know this to be true, for I designed you this way. Just as my Mother is gentle, so too are you, who share her femininity. Come to me and I will help you find it within you.

You are never alone. Did you know this? Though at times you may feel as if it is only you, that could never be true. I am in your heart at all times. Talk to me. Lean on me. I am there.

When you cry, I cry with you. As a father mourns for his children, so I mourn for you. There is not a moment of your sorrow that I have not felt as if it were my own. I love you. Did you know this? Have you forgotten?

I will never change. I will never leave. Who else can say this in earnest? Do not rely on yourself alone. Let me help. Let me lead. I promise I will not abandon you, whatever comes.

No life won't be easy. Your suffering will not vanish. But let me be your strength when you have nothing left. Let me be your hope when you are empty. Let me be everything you need. I long to support you in every moment. Did you know this?

Did you know that you are cherished by me, just as you are, right now and in every stage of your life? I know you better than you know yourself. I knew you before your mother knew you. It was I who willed your existence and sent an angel to be by your side every day that you walked on the earth.

I know there are days when it must feel like I don't care, but I do. I'm sorry that I can't always show you that in the ways you understand, but please know I always care. You have my care, and the care of my Mother, whose arms are open to embrace you at every moment.

My arms are also open: to steady you, to comfort you, to shield you. You need only to fall into them. I am there waiting.

I will always forgive you. Did you know this? No matter what you have done, no matter what you have said, come to me, repent with a sincere heart, and I will forgive. There is nothing so dark that my light cannot penetrate.

I am filled with joy when you talk with me or have any thought towards me. Did you know this? And in case you had forgotten, I'd like to say it again: I love you, gentle woman.

ZC

zelie crafts

zeliecraftsshop.com
handmade
heartfelt

We shall find our little ones again up above

St. Zelie Martin

About the Author and Illustrator

Madeleine Karako is the founder of Zelie Crafts, an online religious store that provides faith-filled items for your home. She graduated from the University of Dallas in 2014 with a BA in English Literature. She now lives with her husband and three children. Her days are filled with caring for her kids, working from home, homeschooling and painting whenever she can. The idea for this book came to her while rocking her newborn, and she hopes it will heal many hearts. You can find more of her work at www.zeliecraftsshop.com.

First Edition: January 2023

ISBN 979-889298005-0   US $30.50
                            53050

9 798892   980050